EXTREME PLACES

COULD YOU LIVE HERE?

Alison Hawes

Crabtree Publishing Company
www.crabtreebooks.com

Author: Alison Hawes
Editor: Crystal Sikkens
Project coordinator: Kathy Middleton
Production coordinator: Ken Wright
Prepress technician: Margaret Amy Salter
Series consultant: Gill Matthews

Picture credits:
Alamy Images: Mediscan/Medical-on-Line 7
Corbis: (Cover) Dean Conger 6, EPA 10, EPA/Wu Hong 15
Dreamstime: Totorean 13r
Getty Images: DigitalGlobe 16
Istockphoto: Juergen Sack 19, Joris Van 12, William Walsh 18
Photolibrary: Oxford Scientific/Ariadne Van Zandbergen 9
Rex Features: Richard Jones 14, K Nomach 8
Shutterstock: (Cover) Vladimir Melnik,
   Robert Paul van Beets 5, Marcus Brown 21,
   Franck Camhi 20, Jules Kitano 13l, Terry Poche 17,
   Jerry Sharp 4, Sia Chen How 11

Every effort has been made to trace copyright holders and to obtain their permission for use of copyright material. The authors and publishers would be pleased to rectify any error or omission in future editions. All the Internet addresses given in this book were correct at the time of going to press. The author and publishers regret any inconvenience caused if addresses have changed or sites have ceased to exist, but can accept no responsibility for any such changes.

Library and Archives Canada Cataloguing in Publication

Hawes, Alison, 1952-
     Extreme places : could you live here? / Alison Hawes.

(Crabtree connections)
Includes index.
ISBN 978-0-7787-9940-5 (bound).--ISBN 978-0-7787-9962-7 (pbk.)

     1. Extreme environments--Juvenile literature.
I. Title. II. Series: Crabtree connections.

GB58.H39 2010   j910   C2010-901512-6

Library of Congress Cataloging-in-Publication Data

Hawes, Alison, 1952-
     Extreme places : could you live here? / Alison Hawes.
          p. cm. -- (Crabtree connections)
     Includes index.
     ISBN 978-0-7787-9962-7 (pbk. : alk. paper) -- ISBN 978-0-7787-9940-5 (reinforced library binding : alk. paper)
     1. Extreme environments--Juvenile literature. I. Title. II. Series.

     GB58.H39 2010
     910--dc22

                                        2010008058

Crabtree Publishing Company
www.crabtreebooks.com   1-800-387-7650

Printed in the U.S.A./062010/WO20100815

Published in Canada
Crabtree Publishing
616 Welland Ave.
St. Catharines, Ontario
L2M 5V6

Published in the United States
Crabtree Publishing
PMB 59051
350 Fifth Avenue, 59th Floor
New York, New York 10118

CONTENTS

LIVING AT EXTREMES

Where do you live? Can you find it on this map?
Many people live in homes and places that
are very different from yours.

Floods occur in parts of
the world where rain falls
heavily and suddenly.

DID YOU KNOW?

The people who live in the
places marked on this map
live in some of the **harshest
environments** on Earth.

The driest
inhabited
place on Earth

Atacama Desert

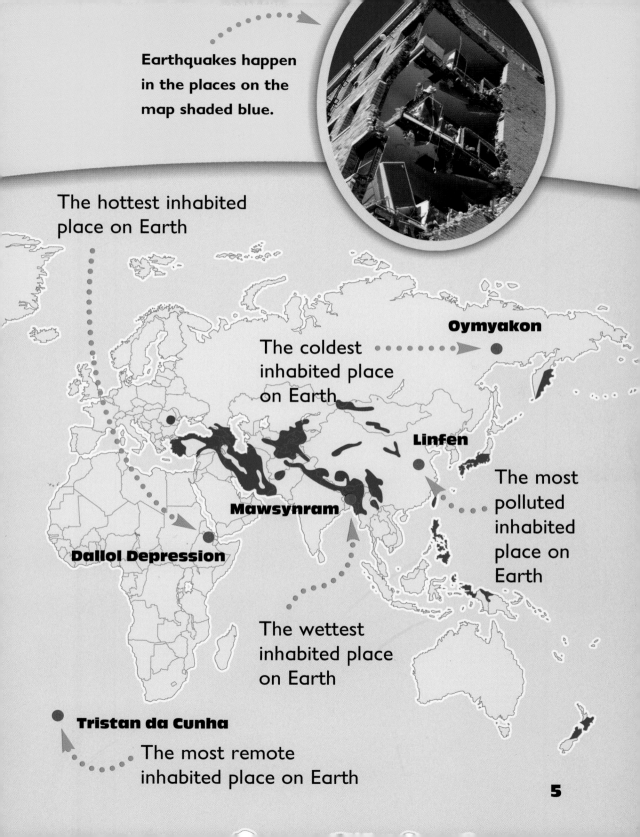

Earthquakes happen in the places on the map shaded blue.

The hottest inhabited place on Earth

Oymyakon

The coldest inhabited place on Earth

Linfen

The most polluted inhabited place on Earth

Mawsynram

Dallol Depression

The wettest inhabited place on Earth

Tristan da Cunha

The most remote inhabited place on Earth

5

THE COLDEST PLACE ON EARTH

Oymyakon is a small village in Russia. The temperature in Oymyakon can be three times as cold as your freezer! Oymyakon is the coldest inhabited place on Earth.

The temperature in Oymyakon is often −58°F (−50°C), or lower!

°F
20°
10°
0°
-10°
-20°
-30°
-40°
-50°
-60°
-70°

The houses in Oymyakon have steep roofs to keep the snow off.

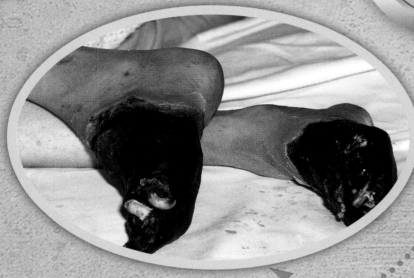

Frostbite **has caused many people in Oymyakon to lose their fingers and toes.**

TOO COLD TO FARM

The ground is too cold and hard to grow much food. So, villagers live mostly on horse and reindeer meat.

AMAZING

When it is −58°F (−50°C):

Cell phones do not work

Pens do not work

Diesel fuel freezes

THE HOTTEST PLACE ON EARTH

The Dallol **Depression**, in Africa, is a place of rocks, volcanoes, and **salt flats**. The Afar people live here. They are called **nomads**.

The Dallol Depression is the hottest inhabited place on Earth.

The temperature in the Dallol Depression is often 94°F (34°C).

THE WORKING DAY

The Afar women walk miles every day to find water. The Afar men cut and sell the salt from the salt flats.

The Afar people live in huts made from palm mats and sticks. They can be folded up when the people move.

The Afar people live on meat, milk, and cheese from their goats.

THE WETTEST PLACE ON EARTH

Mawsynram is a small village in India. More rain falls here in one day than some places get in a whole year! It is the wettest inhabited place on Earth.

DID YOU KNOW?

A knup is a waterproof covering shaped like a giant shell. It is worn by people in Mawsynram to keep them dry as they work in the rain.

This man is wearing a knup as he picks crops in a field.

Rice plants need a lot of water to grow. A lot of rice is grown in Mawsynram!

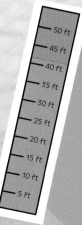

Mawsynram has almost 42 feet (13 m) of rain in a year.

MONSOON WEATHER

On **monsoon** days, the villagers may have to change their wet clothes many times.

THE DRIEST PLACE ON EARTH

The Atacama **Desert** in Chile is a place of sand, dust, and rocks. It has not rained in some parts of the Atacama for over 400 years!

The Atacama gets only about ⅟₃₂ of an inch (1 mm) of rain a year.

1 inch

¾ inch

½ inch

¼ inch

The Atacama Desert is the driest place on Earth.

DESERT HOMES

Some people live in **oasis** villages in the middle of the desert.

San Pedro is an oasis village built with adobe bricks. Adobe bricks keep the houses cool.

Big pipes carry water to towns in the desert.

I DON'T BELIEVE IT!
Some villagers put up nets to catch the fog. The fog drips into pipes, which take the water to the village.

DID YOU KNOW?
Mummies of people who lived thousands of years ago have been found in the Atacama Desert.

THE MOST POLLUTED PLACE ON EARTH

Linfen is a big city in China. The air in Linfen is often filled with thick, black dust.

DID YOU KNOW?

Many people in Linfen have breathing problems because of the pollution.

Linfen is one of the most polluted cities on Earth.

FUEL

Coal is a very important fuel in China. The dust and **smog** come from the coal mines and factories in and around Linfen.

People in Linfen often wear face masks when they go out.

GOOD NEWS!

Some polluting factories in Linfen are being shut down.

I DON'T BELIEVE IT!
Linfen is so polluted you cannot see the stars at night.

THE MOST REMOTE PLACE ON EARTH

Tristan da Cunha is an island in the Atlantic Ocean. Its nearest neighbors are more than 1,000 miles (1,600 km) away! Tristan da Cunha is the most remote place on Earth.

I DON'T BELIEVE IT!
The islanders finally got television in 2001, but they only have one channel.

This photograph of Tristan da Cunha was taken from above.

ISLAND LIFE

About 270 people live on the island. They sell stamps and crayfish to people overseas to make a living. The mail takes a long time to arrive, and there is no way to get to a hospital quickly.

Crayfish live in the waters around the island.

DID YOU KNOW?

The islanders share:
- one school;
- one police officer;
- one doctor;
- one swimming pool;
- and eight surnames between them!

LIVING IN AN EARTHQUAKE ZONE

Big earthquakes can be dangerous.
Many people live in places
where big earthquakes happen.

**Earthquakes happen
when the Earth's
crust moves.**

**I DON'T
BELIEVE IT!**
There is an
earthquake somewhere
in the world about
every 11 seconds!

DID YOU KNOW?

Earthquake-proof houses are sometimes built with hollow bricks. They cause less damage than solid bricks if they fall and hit someone.

KILLER QUAKE!

Big earthquakes can destroy homes and kill people. People in earthquake zones do what they can to keep themselves safe.

Some people try to build earthquake-proof homes.

19

LIVING IN A FLOOD ZONE

Rivers and oceans can cause floods. Too much water can be dangerous. Big floods can destroy homes and kill people.

DANGER

Floods can also destroy
- crops and animals
- roads and bridges
- power lines
- factories and stores

This dam stops the Nile River from flooding every year.

FLOOD ZONES

Some people in flood zones build homes that will not wash away in a flood.

DID YOU KNOW?

Waste is often caught up in flood water. Diseases can be caught by drinking the dirty water.

This house is built on stilts to keep it above a flood.

GLOSSARY

adobe Sundried clay or mud bricks

crust The top layer of the Earth's surface

depression A low-lying area of land

desert A dry area of land that has little rain

environment The conditions of the world around you

frostbite When parts of the body are injured by extreme cold

harsh Very difficult. A place that is very difficult to live in is often described as harsh

inhabited A place in which people live

monsoon A wind that brings very heavy rain

mummy A body that has been treated and wrapped in cloth so it will not decay quickly

nomads People who move from place to place in search of food and water

oasis A place in a desert where water is found

salt flats Dried-up saltwater lakes

smog Mixture of fog and smoke

FURTHER INFORMATION

Web sites

Find out about different people and places around the world at:
http://kids.nationalgeographic.com/Places/Find

Discover more about earthquakes, floods, or extreme weather at:
www.fema.gov/kids/dizarea.htm

Find out about the places children live all over the world at:
www.katw.org/index.cfm

Books

Homes Around the World series by Nicola Barber. Crabtree Publishing
Company (2008)

Earthquakes by Franklyn M. Branley. Collins (2008)

Earthquake Alert! by Shilpa Mehta-Jones. Crabtree Publishing Company
(2004)

Flood and Monsoon Alert! by Rachel Eagen. Crabtree Publishing
Company (2005)

INDEX